FIREBREAK

FIREBREAK

POEMS BY

DAVID WEVILL

*'A strip of ploughed or cleared land made
to check the spread of a prairie or forest
fire'*

MACMILLAN
ST MARTIN'S PRESS

© David Wevill 1971

SBN boards: 333 12356 5
SBN paper: 333 12357 3

Library of Congress Catalog Card No: 76–160136

First published 1971 *by*
MACMILLAN LONDON LTD
London and Basingstoke
Associated companies in New York Toronto
Dublin Melbourne Johannesburg & Madras

Printed in Great Britain by
WESTERN PRINTING SERVICES LTD
Bristol

For Sharon

List of Contents

'You have both fought well. Therefore, Ploughman,
yours be the honor; yours, Death, the victory
Each man owes his life to Death, his body to
earth, his soul to Us'

No
    my soul to myself
to the new one
who will come
              or will not come

body/
      to earth, yes
to the one who
has come

        mine to hers

'from the bird's quill
I take my plough'

Night/Day

As dream corrects
the facts of daylight
what cries in me

is no bird
              but some chirping nerve
nested in fear
scrabbling at the fly-screens –
                 'sickness unto death'
in the black
January night

             But the good
body returns
          unbroken
edged like glass
            falling through years
without air

to irrigate a desert
make drinking water from the sea

calms itself
        by numbers
through each of which passes the cell

of a baby's first eyes

widening
to ask
and find

How being dense
the world
        sudden windows
open
from sun
beyond sun

the tooled wheels
of clocks
      spinning into the stars, all
   in an eye
rags of cloud
and mists with high velocities

to fear
or give praise

a mirror beams you in

you are what
a stone
can't think itself

but is

            which is the way
the wind
travels
    the eye
when the mind lets loose from all

that is
not
it —

a red rock
with a green vein
            the toward and into and
out
away from

things,

            or is it time
the shudder of birds against the seasons
                        mating
only with the egg
of hours

the
bass
string . . .

tell me where I should take you beyond
this
        all things
diminishing

for they will say
'inhuman'
when you mean 'I'm trying to find'

and there is law
in what they say
                and in you
opinion or faith
only

and
anguish

a minor chord
just off the point of things

but strongly played

earth, the lover
not God
          or man
with his fire-brain

or storms on the moon

obvious
          but what
tomorrow might have changed

a thing
made useful
               no longer itself
life
compressed
into crystals
               'I am
the beginning and the end'

preserve
the leaf

               x-ray
               the dead

that is what life
looked like

               as the stars look now

                        and in you
        opinion or faith
          only

        and
        anguish
                    and wonder
        in things
                    you can't scale or change

        between us, and when
        the new one comes

        touch its face
                        to find me

Poem

        A year
        burning away time.

        Where are the words?

        The room
        was full of people,
        but they didn't speak.

        A year
        without love or hate —

        no natural
        cleansing or disfigurement —

lying awake,
watching the car lights play
and the branched wind wash the walls, until life

is another form of time
without substance, breathing.

America.
One more rash of lights
in an interminable orbit. Round

and round,
the earth, the moon –

praying for that innocence now
which must keep talking,

or stops forever.

For Nefertiti

As if a shark
could become the sea it fished
my mind swirled
in a blood dissolve –
legs, toes, hair, eyes
thrashed in a bubble –
'Air! Air! . . .'

But the one who came with a lamp
could not sing my soul into the other world.

I lay awake all night
prodded by nurses
squares
of grey daylight
revived
a world of things to touch

To learn to use
mirrors cautiously now
knowing what is behind them, how

cold the water feels
how old the toothbrush –
junk in the cupboard, belonging to no one
until this body
                    reclaims it, accepts it
becomes it
like a second skin (but unnerved

forever numb on the surface now)
the tame hands
trembling, not yet mine

O seed born in the sun
whose life I replace
whose name I was given at birth, and
by accident, still have.

November

It is a cold understanding, and lonely
to steal on the spirit, asleep
and find a stranger there –
some stone drunk
who wobbled in
crashed your hospitality, took your wife

And you stand
throwing knives
into a statue of wood
                  the Buddha –

to kill the spirit
your ideal
that sleeping face

Leaves fall early, are gone by daylight

Alone in the abandoned room
                        November windows.

It

The snake enters the house.
The house receives it.

The snake feels at home
stretches, curls
gets itself some food.

The snake and the house
feed on each other,

grow together
feed each other
in permanent darkness.

No visitors. Blood
tastes black
temperature warm, constant –
beat of the unseen sun.

From the net of nerves
head, hands and feet.

Movement, disproportion
neither alive nor dead
but undefinable. Now

touched by whispers
gurglings
drain sounds
waste noises
                    afflatus
of light and air –

                    tensed
to break the blood-lock
ark of all creatures
mud, community, pain –

and always cold
always seeking a home.

Snapshots

From the tallest building on earth
a boy flies his toy red plane

It flutters over New York
        tiny crimson consciousness
death wish

refusing the wind

   II
Over the Grand Canyon
a hundred faces
                    tick of locusts
the great ash pit
purpling of flame through the haze
at sunset

voices like dustfalls

distance
        no echo

the heart in the body too small

   III
Montana a sea of rain
to the sulphur of Yellowstone
                            wet snow
terror of the moon
the pines
        the skull-white lake
                        listening

Drive all night
rather than live cold dreams

Taos

Hills become trees

horses become trees

the wind whickers,   a chestnut
colt, caught
                    in the barbwire

as the men
ride the mare away   uphill

Teacher

Weaving among the other placards, at a point where the crowd
is thinnest, a bright red banner with a green scrawl, 'Death to
Mutants'. The red stands out startlingly, the color of a poked
eye, against the cardboard and flesh, green trees and smoke-white
and glass office façades. The boy who carries it, as I crane to
look, is tall, very tall. He has a beard and glasses thick as diver's
goggles. He is almost twice as tall as the crowd, pale and long
haired, raised like a crucifixion above the crowd. The crowd is
pressing him. He moves, a strange slow loping shuffle, like a
giraffe, as if attached by wires to all the other limbs, and talking
to himself, or wetting his mouth, or chewing gum. He does not
look as if he likes what he's doing, was paid to do it, or forced to.
The little group pushing him is singing a familiar tune, and as
they come closer I catch the words

Two headed pig, five legged calf
Wolf-boy chimp-man lives cut in half
Keep them away, kill them today
If the state don't do it WE'LL ALL HAVE TO PAY

shrieking the last phrase, girls' voices hysterical high. The little procession goes past. The police charge and break us up. People picking bits of camera out of their faces, placards falling as if a bulldozer scythed through them, eyes that smiled with what little tolerance the world had taught them suddenly squinting screwed up with hate and terror, girls trapped in a stampede of horns. The giant drifts off by himself still carrying his placard, down some alley, still masticating his cud of gum, faster, faster. Who is he? When I was selling hamburgers at the Fair one summer, there was a giant in a stall who never said a word, just sat still or stood, with the faraway eyes of Prometheus. Weak heart, liver, kidneys, spine, stomach, bladder, bones, eyes. You couldn't get to him. He was fading, fading as I looked. The cops stand in little groups counting the money they have stolen from pockets, passports, identity cards, sleeping pills, family pictures, scribbled poems. No one gets arrested these days. The situation between the police and the people is called the Truce of Attila. The police are out for blood and plunder, the jails are empty. The police grow their hair long and carry rawhide whips, the hospitals are full. I make my way after the giant, down the alley. I find his placard in a garbage can, but the alley is empty, the square of grey light beyond it is empty. In the dim light the psychedelic colors of cracked tenement windows and cars. A little joy gone wrong, the earth color missing, replaced by ozones of the mind as the earth retreats from us and space yawns. No longer possible to tell who is behind what, for the state has turned the tables on us, has stolen our personae and masks, our battle-cries, and the blacks have been quiet for ten years. I look to right and left. I am alone, a Warsaw ghost, the high singing of wind fluting in the half open windows of glass buildings overhead, choirs of the dead. I teach three courses at the city college. My lectures go down well but no one listens. My best friends are a dead wife, a living wife, and that boy, the giant, whom I hope to get to know. How can I wash this blood off my hands?

Market Square

In the store window
behind yellow glass
two .38's, two .45's
      (one with a hand-stitched holster)
a blackjack, a row of flick-knives

all cheap at the price

ammunition boxed among
the dead wasps and flies
gunmetal, nickel plate
wood rubbed smooth and eaten into by sweat

such as shines
on the passing, reflected faces
who pause here . . .
                And pause
at the store's other half

where behind the yellowing glass
the brothers Kennedy and Martin Luther King
stare beyond their portraits
blindly into the sun

their eyes not meeting the eyes

and an Easter message scrawled
in the same hand
that fixed the price on the guns –

'Brothers, remember and pray'

Indian Mission, San Antonio

Chief Seattle never knew
his city
        but said, the dead never die
we are the ghosts of the old land

the burnt-out motel
        the flowering garden of wrecks
are failures of the
front-brain

        So it might have been
Victorio or Cochise who burnt the city in '89
ghosts of the dead
        buried but unappeased

each with his spear
in the side of a timber christ
        too weak to move

The lovely missions were dead
dead from the start
        If this one lives
it is through the tensions of ghosts
who never knew each other's hearts
        or could tell

substance from shadow

the dark hidden tree-grain
the crippled façade of saints
                            gone blind in the sun.

Southern January

An army advancing into a mirror.
'I felt the two worlds. And at once'
Eyes and hair
Night of the singing roots.

Make
        no idols of the flesh,
The air you breathe is deaths and other lives.
Grass shares us, the bluejay and the piston engine –
Our cries
Dissolve the gods.

What answers the drilled atoms
Flash along the wires –
Stars to be known without being touched,
Radiation fogs of sight closing into sound,
Debussy, the night flower,
                            thermal
Worm of silence,
                staves of motion,
                                cries.

Somehow we eat.
And when we cannot sleep, we feed on light.
The armies have no one to fight –

They wade in memories, like a man
Returned to his childhood summers,
Hunting for life in the colorless salt blood.

1969

Rimbaud
multiplied by millions

the inner voice
moves out into the sun

Plato's cave is empty

and earth has a green
center again –

red yellow black and white
the edges of vision

a single eye oil rainbow floating on water

2.
Blood is the water. Visions edged
in black and white
scream for their green center –

yellow and red
are armies fighting
lockjaw for life –

and the cave is full of noise
decibels deeper than sound –
the inner voice crawls to the dark where

16

Rimbaud
shrinks to zero . . .

death . . . gangrene

Emblem

A man's incandescent skeleton between my eye and the sun.
The atoms burnt through it, a bare, charred heat for
silhouette.

Noble words a smoke ring of flame.
Rhetoric a whisper light years beyond things known.

That gap in the pelvic bone where his race created itself.
Those eyes which saw through time images of god and reason,
gone.

Pestered now by meteors, some malarial, others with stings
like horseflies.

Hells Angels are roaring through space. Smoking rubber in the
glass-clear cold airless well, where no sacrifice feels
the black knife slip his heart.

A bare, charred heat for silhouette –
Go, go, filaments, go, of the burnt skeleton.

Lose no sleep over this dream of re-entry into the condom of
daylight and dust. Here the moon's vulva opens. The Sea of
Tranquility is a dripping cave where blind shell creatures,
colorless, crawl.

In the clear cooling pool the skeletons will harden again,
both male and female.

We wake washed in the sweat where all seas meet.
Bone to bone, our breath sifting through our ribs like wind.

Texan Spring

Headlights in the mirror on a lonely road
frost-still in the warm moonlight

I begin to wonder who my killer is
crawling through deep, dry sand in the craters of
my footsteps
on a bottom of solid glass
skidding, searching past
the light-stabs
in the heart

No one, love
just distance
The high beam with a warning light
and a horizon of dulled silver
where trees pray eternally to the winds
lapping the sea at their roots
inland
so far from water
the engine sucking us on

As I am
and as you are
flesh a time-bomb, acorn packed with fire

weasels in their chimneys

solid beef digesting in the rancher's gut.

Death Valley

          desert fingers
          counting beads, old
          spark plugs

          her hair
          brushes my feet, sifts
          like spiders

          the long knife in my hand
          turned on me
                turned on you

                        you

          we
          know you, you
          filed the flesh from my bones
          give it back, I
          sign my checks in your
          blood but
          where
                is the in-
          terest
          you
          owe
          me

I
looked for
America, let
America come and get me

girl at my feet, go
KILL
my voice flat in your eyes

one life will atone
for every ruined pore in my skin

the pigs
must die, the poor

vomit air

inherit God

                    I
am the son
of man,
in the manger you broke me, turned

my cry into words
my touch to trust

all my women, you
blind as to day or night, assassins
with burnt-out eyes

                    they will
kiss you
as none have kissed me

as the snake
kisses,

have sucked
my poison
to spit it into your blood

through lips
cracked, so they will
die too
                    yes, they will
find you

whoever

my forty days

in whatever
bed
denied
me

by
the
cross

Human Universe?

SPACE may be the fact
as Olson says

reach, not intensity
the lick of air on the skin, no worm

in the bone marrow
being God—

that space is our fire, not hell
begin looking: these bones

yes they sing –
and the song is of life and truth

for these are movements,
fore and back in time

and across lands and oceans
in flight from our shadows, the cave

II
But are my eyes the world?
The living turned to the sun

held a mirror up to her face
in the cave, coaxed

light back,
first on the sea,

then on these islands, slow
as a year in the chapters of rock

and the ice
crept back to the poles leaving

scarred rock, no promises
not even now

III
Tell me what spirit
born lost will not answer

that light is the pure gift
light and speech, now

sea and the sea's coast,
lost, found. Memory crawls

o snail,
your house is motion

self, searching for its world
touched, not tamed, raped, but unopened

Two lives has Venus,

one at dawn

and one at evening.

Atitlán

Do you hear this my friend
down there

where the stars call to the sun -
                    jaguar, prowls the night
                              without shadow

your blood is the river he tracks
from the water-void
                    came animals and plants

and man created from mud
                    to mud returns

and men made of wood without minds
                    destroyed by slash and burn

then flesh –
frail, but of flesh
                made, they melt
in the black rains and floods of the long year

This whisper
keeps the potency of time,
to hold all possible but that which
                                    dies in you

of long absence

or, returning to find
the place just as you left it

a bird, a lake, the profile of three mountains

afraid your breathing might anger
the spirits of welcome and death

This is your birth place

You come with clean hands, whom

the flood waters
                drowned

now
grain
revives

In the *Bardos*, to catch the moment when
                        breath dies, breath returns
be patient

listen, don't speak

For Woodwinds

The dry wind ticks in the leaves
The coral snake has left his hole by the water pail
The days climb to a hush
oven noon, and at night
the hidden river leaves a lake in the cup of your belly
where
we dabble like children, lights out
to the small wild noises in the grass
and the dead eye of the gun in the bedside drawer

II
Some mornings
the sea returns. Our valley of air
alive with sunshapes, shed scales
solders our lungs with the plumb pressure of tons
                              of dark water
No life
        no appetite
But sap drips from the sun into our eyes
                        staining the dust
The cardinal high in his tree
warns of the snake's return

III
Juniper green on electric blue
enduring while the first leaves fall
and the road subliminal, grey
grainy film of a dead river, goat bones, glass
glitters through dust
                    More dead
and many wounded. They cry for time
to tell us what to live for, not to die for –
the old who would take us with them over the river,
lacking the blood we drown in.

Prelude: The Giant

The light tells me, I have woken up too early again. Or it is just the glow of the city thrown on the clouds. I can't tell. Light is light, and it wakes me. I sleep less and less deeply anyway.

Today is my birthday.

Why should I be afraid of the light? Night and day are the same thing. Whatever is here by night is here by day and the hands on my watch cover the same hours. In the light I see my shadow. At night I cannot tell where I begin and end. Or if I begin and end.

It seems I've been a long time coming out of that womb. Inching through it, like a goat digesting in a python, shit and all, bones cracking, spine bent double. Daylight filters through the stretched skin and scales. To be excreted as dirt. A little mucous sack of crushed bones, would about be it. Little. Everything is little. Do people feel pain?

Light.
It is my birthday.
I am twenty one.

When the doctor saw me last he said, Jack, you're not eating enough. I took it as a joke and answered, Doctor, I'm eating them out of house and home already. But he was serious. Look, feel those ribs. You're becoming transparent. Your heart is strong enough to take a bit more weight. Six hundred? I suggested. At least that, and light exercises to convert it to gristle so's you won't need that stick ALL the time. You lie around too much. I feel weak, it's the effort, the light, seeing my shadow. In the mornings I feel sick. Only in the afternoons, under the umbrella, lying in the shallow pool, reading, I'm at my best. Do you ever think of girls? he asked, and smiled. When you are nine feet tall you do not have passion.

Light.

Interplanetary travel.

I'd like that. To go to the stars before they come to me. The

stars and I have darkness in common. But they have space, and an uncommonly long existence. I feel closer to them than I feel to people. At dawn they disappear, and I am left with people. I sleep less and less. It seems as if there is someone passing back and forth, back and forth, across my room all night long. It is not Doctor, or Ma or Pa, or my sister Benny (she's at school). It must be someone I invented. A line growing on a graph chart, tracing itself out, in the shape of a man. He is purple, like iodine or blood in a bad light. But I can hear him breathe. And sometimes a singing like I heard in the sea off Maine at night, age ten, when Benny was eight and boy-crazy for the fishermen. It is a man, and his head is bowed. He is never aware of me. He is thinking. I watch the light through the windows, the clear starlight, or the light reflected upward on the clouds. The stars tell of long lives. I would like to be of the race of the stars.

But it's daylight.
It is my birthday.
I am twenty one.

Nodes

Dancing
    on a string
string
dance
    dancing
string
string

Babel's eyes, shrewd, weary
crossed by a smoke of thought
                    salamander, rabbit, mole
Death
withdrew the water that reflects the fire

II

Too many had come too close

Who in his time has not dreamed
worse devils than there are
                                    yet
never suffered?

Do the priests
who control us feel the fire of their own knives?

III

We dance on the same nerve
Odessa
        horses threading the dust
the length of the sun

pierced by a flying straw

A rootless acrobat

turned farmer
                    engineer
killer
for the sake of life

IV

There was a junction. Two trains met. They fought.

The death of the Admiral
in the snow
                by the frozen lake
left bones in my garden

Those closest
come from far away,
those I have never known
eat with me at my table.

    V
They lie buried
They lie buried

Peace to the bones
Peace to the killers

The water is cold and deep
There we meet
                each face a star

Reflecting

A Beginning

First this house
it is not mine
it has no roof
it has no walls

the house is just a frame

I lie where the winds blow across me

Second, the land
I do not own it
east west and south
canyon and snow mountains

to the north a sloping field

I walk where I am the only hunger

Thirdly, yourself
I possess but do not
possess
            animal
slow as the seasons
caught in the long count of the blood

we roof the house
we nail the walls

we walk in the company of our shadows

Through Arizona

Not quite daybreak but near enough
early splendour of highways

light
on the high snow: light
                        behind us
fallen trees
wars —

radio gone dead

Land purchase: $15 down
                    $15 a month, how
sudden
pacing it out,
red earth, sage, juniper, mountain grass

one comes home, is
a figure here; part of the land
                    impromptu human
devil
or god

with water rights
right of possession, right of house

to live
to die
to move on!

Let the Light

Let the light come to you slowly.
A place where moss has formed
after the holocaust –

Not metal burning in the sun
or holy fire
or a cup touched by acid
or the radiant tortoise egg.

Begin
to time yourself against this light,
wake in your own hands.

I've
drunk water from your lips.
The well heals.

The well heals, and
still we may drown in it
or the water suddenly leap into fire

our kiss become the lip of the scorpion

Two Rooms

One room newly painted white
Four windows like sails to the winds

At night
            stillness or thunder
Starlight above the half curtains.
                                    No
                memory this room; just

Sunlight and needles of wind
Through the nail-holes in the old white boards.

This is the room where we lie together
You and I, outside time.

                        The other room
Was burnt out. Like Izanami it died
In agony giving birth to the god of fire

Decomposes quietly under its
Coal of rafters
                    brooding, black and empty
                    in the underworld.

We do not think of this other room
But the memory of fire
Returns to us in the wind and starlight

Hangs above our heads
                         like the moon
In Klee's 'Stars Above Evil Houses'.
                                        And

Fear is evil
Our fear

For here we must live
Between

The white room and the burnt-out room
Between time's cinder and no-time

In the bed our bodies make
In the snow and fire of our love.

The Stopped Heart

Your nerves yes your hair
like fire through a copper filter
spread over me
heartbeats of fire

There are always
telephones
knocks on the door
laughter in bars
eyes watching us. And

the crimson mudcake of the Texas sunset
(eating our portion, each
 the seed of the other)
is also an eye within us –

ram's horn clouds, aureole
around the fiery cyclops.
Eyes watching eyes
see only night and questions, the dark

inside you where
the flickering tongue of the seed
searches your breath, the briefest death
comes on us both

And this is where
the starlight
jumps like a spark

between your eyes and mine

a million dust worlds singeing like pepper
as infinite as the pores
which body inherits from body
and passes on

Between the two of me
and the two of you
or more, the helix

invisible at both ends
is all fire and heat and chameleon heaving the air
in gulps like ocean coiled

around the rod of fire
such light
we pass into negative, our bones
show, and our hair
has whitened a thousand years

As if
the afterlife receives us
as we are, no questions, into the
dusk-nerve, where our eyes
wander without bodies

Never alone
and aware of the world
seeking us, calling us

Radar and flowers
the germ
that hibernates in the grain of sand

lifeless, voiceless, total.

Cardinal

He comes in the night between us
the red bird of blood
cocks its tail

                    We live
for years in the shadow of one night
knowing
          afraid to know
          why do you ask
                              what
contempt makes me answer

The sun shallows in the juniper wood, I
sing to myself
                    I shave with words
I eat a red-eyed breakfast egg
you spill the shower over the floor

Now can we begin as the sun drums in the leaves
thinking of time and the false role of the mind
                                        controlling it

more substance
than essence

                    that what the red bird asks
is the death of us both
and the life of us both

so we may return
hand in hand
walking among thorns

knowing that where our feet touch is the earth
knowing that where our feet touch is ourselves.

Aquarius

If the past has been
a coming together, as with our cells
and life is a second coming
of the self born of the cells,
then I am becoming, we
have not arrived at each other yet

II

But see through each other like glass back
through our past incarnations
second by second. Dreams
come as messengers
bringing us news of the dead

III

and the abandoned. As
metals exchange their atoms from
long touching, their
cells are in us. Do not
weep for the dead who breathe your air

IV

they
are our variant selves now,
free of time. When you come to my hands
I touch you, like the air –
when I come to your hands
I am the air you touch

V

And the angel comes to free me from
the locked room –

what I have done and not done
is bread of me, melting in your
waters, my voices
are cries from my skin where your waters
dismember, dissolve and enter

VI

touching
the different colors
of pain, healing those
who suffered and died and those
who lived to hate and still
cry for that body which is no longer mine

VII

no longer
shit and stuffing
to feed their spirits –
no sacrifice of theirs or they
of ours. And the angel comes
bringing us word of his love, if we will listen.

Three

I have known three healers
    one, a dead woman
    nearer than anyone
she left to inhabit a tree, under
       the snow I will not meet her
not now

Another was a man
    a greying haired child
    whose vanities were small, his love

a need of love
                bewildered by the world
he loved and feared

You are the third, the one of pure chance
        my wife
                by being no more
than you are. May autumn and the night
                        winds cool your fever, now
quiet house
                green blanket
sleep.

Echo

When I entered your house I left
my footprints. The child
leaves the house
in his father's tracks

Our trails will cross
at all points in his life
the seasons leading him
through dust, rain, mud and snow

But the dimension of distance will be
an unclimbed hill
a sea-bed without
his footprints or mine, this

taking him longest
to understand. You and I

will forget
or something will forget us
though you swear not. Out of our dream
he came
his lightning woke us. Time
will blind him to our bodies

I have gone on, you continue
and he grows. The clock
is in his hands. I am the stopped hand
of hours he has already forgotten.

Dead One

Who comes knocking

     Worm comes knocking

Countersign

Muffled winter above me. Neither the sounds of the gardener
nor the heavy feet of the wreathlayers. Your signal was to shake
the small tree whose root nudges my left side. Nothing happened.
I can't tell your feet from any other. My nipple doesn't rise to
your hand carressing my stone; nor do I squirm when your hand
rakes the length of my grass. Your voice humming is no more
human than the wind. You come and go, I know you come and
go, but when you have stopped coming and going I will not
know that, it could be any other, or no one. Our code did not
work. We are cut off forever. You do not know I think, if this
is thinking, or feel pain is this is pain I feel. These numbers
occur to me.

```
7   31    2     5    47   074   99
      11    1    57    3   999
            15   12    9
                 00
```

There is no pattern. They are coefficients of nothingness. You will sell me into print, or in conversation drop your eyes, reach for another cigarette, betray yourself only in dreams when the hot sheet bunched between your legs stiffens to a dead name. And I do not know any of this. Not for sure. You are a photograph existing in many poses, a quality of light heightened, faded, darkened. Without sunlight only the negative. Your raincoat smelling of many London rains, torn under the left arm from pulling a kitten out of a tree. Or have you gotten all smart and dandied yourself up a bit? I might as well be talking to myself, and that's no change. You were always a silent worshipper at the temple of death. Thorns, the lake dry in March, the long wooden bridge fading in haze to the village where the headman's radio played loudly to the cattle, and the pagodas were full of cowshit, thorns, flies. The ambassador pissed on the wall and said, this country needs irrigation. If you stood above me pissing long enough a drop of you might filter through to me. I pray for such desecration. As God's bride, I don't get it very often. Do you want to know how He does it? He comes in the form of a cold worm, a tapeworm, of infinite length, a solitaria, prying me open, like a thread passing through the gills of a fish. And while He's doing it with me He's doing it with all the other dead women in christendom, nondenominationally, in all their ages and states, from the Virgin Mary to Wee Susan, age nine months, cholera, Mandalay, 1887. I do not meant to taunt you in your helplessness. Since God is male the men are rather hard-up down here. Make it good while you can. Better to be lost at sea and picked apart by sharks. My body misses you. I feel useless, a time capsule sealed in to myself, an item in the memories of busy friends. Look, I will invent a life of you, knowing nothing. It will be a better life than you can live, more consistent, because in it you will not change or age or forget. You will go about the world with my sign marked on your face, so people will know you and know me through you. And you will come to no harm as long as you are alone, and do not attempt to hide the sign from anyone. Is it a bargain?

Ich liebe dich
        Ich liebe dich
                Ich

Prayer

In the absence of father or god
bless this son

That his eyes will know the details of our lives
                              one day
that created him –

not in the white bitter light
of the empty temple
                    wind, stone or myth

But in the bargain
he must make with his heart
to free himself of all fears not his own
                      not kin to his cry

That his temple be filled
with people and beasts
he can trust without taming

That the horns and water of his birth
guide him through the two worlds

42

belief in self
belief in things

And finally, give him the nerve
to face his own failure
                              the darker face
behind the face in the mirror

which is his substance, all else being ghost.

Forgotten

The gift book borrowed back is the giver's
sacrifice

            Love
like a lime-green beetle in the lamplight
                              after car-hours
the quick edge of pain
of a trapped moth
                  and your hunger

hammering the black dust-grey glass
to get in
            like Cathy's hands

tonight's blood
clotting before dawn

Read these pages: midnight sealed them shut

Neither your brain nor mine can own these words.

Brides I

It is all so stupid
It is nothing

Who suffers but man
Creatures go deeper

    escape, avoid

The old and new
are absurd in my self
and in you

'Meaningless' he wrote
Whose death did he mean

    yours, mine

but probably his own.

Brides II

Whether they kill tomorrow or today
is an adjustment in the volume of
the radiogram . . .

            Angels
after dark are cicadas
or moths weeping around lamps
like a race really concerned about
the loss of God

        . . . in the volume of
the word 'love' in the latest hit
in your light step
on the grass mat

Torn between despair and happiness
where do the windows lead
where does the stair

Behind your eyes
the sirens rise and fall . . .
an adjustment in the volume of dark is the sun

                    And tomorrow
the sea-green leaves
will bake in the south wind
you or the bluejay will wake me
I will bring the coffee

dark as your eyes.

Nocturnes

The lake's banked fires
hiss at the water brim

Words spoken at dusk
                    still echo
nothing wilder than fish

Only the cricket stirs
a warning in the reed-beds

footsteps of a ghost

II

Calm after the accident the cars
melt in the crimson siren
of blood
              Between its stone cliffs
bent like a broken bone

the road lingers, watching

the pine trees tilt their faces at the stars

III

I dream of the coral snake
and you, your body in its Indian silence

brushed by grass
the sweet green stain

padding over stones
hand in hand, towards the dark river
                                        the hidden moon

Her Guardians

They are silent now
as a bud is silent

You are their secret, they
enfold you
as a bud enfolds the cold flower

46

Even the sun can't break
the bud's grip
                until that cell
the bud's brain
kisses you free

Then they will give you up to the wind and rain

Remembering the Monsoon

An incandescent crack of door
in the baked light,

the monsoon's temper gone –
the stones settle in place,

creatures in a daze, rustling after
food and sex. A broad highway coming of age

in the afterlight of rain,
whispers of paintwork fading in the false

winter of the tropics. How
long ago now?
                It comes to me
that time echoes itself
only in the occasional fall of stones,

that flesh absorbs all noises.
Air, where it touches the skin

is only a blind window; and the scorpion sting
delayed, strikes late but deep,

long after the rain's
tenth year has dried –

and that we were there
only confirms that the place is there.

Memorial I

In a time of mock funerals and
pagan prayers for the living,
your death was real.

When there is nothing to mourn but
the future, how can we go on
laying wreaths at your feet?

You spoke of love; but the World
Collective, the collective word
would never understand. You spoke of love,

O, the hole in the breath
like a blessed egg, stillborn
with blood in its eye. You were a winter fury

cursing the lovers
your cold
drove together for warmth . . . Pity

the dead telephone
whispering in your ear
stories of others; and the sun

trying to enter through your frosted window
gave only a bright cold,
a vivid shield of hell.

After you died
they lied about your beauty;
the sun melted everything into the sea.

And they will go on casting your bones
relentlessly, in the wines of many thanksgivings,
until the living find your dying words.

Memorial II

I visited your grave
too often in dreams
while you were still alive

Now I do not want to touch
the real body and the real grass
see the real trees

        Because
your voice will begin to describe
the leaves, the ladybugs
roots as they are
        the germ of wind
that reaches you
flowers, your neighbours' names

the same voice
that claimed and exclaimed so often
such things, your eyes
        quicker than mine
         still quicker than mine

X4

Fell into a false sleep – woke up
there were clouds smoking across the stars
white clouds

and a wind in the room
the room alert, the curtains alive
in their night-dance

My northern friend, asleep by the East River
My southern friend, asleep by the lake of mountains

No one comes,
no one goes

II

The crisis is to tell it as it
happened, before it escapes
                – the news of her death,
and of a new love come, my water-bearer,
time beginning

So little the self
so crude
        without much love or pity

The sea goes deeper than the soul
She is one of the sea's voices, having met no soul
worth living for

And you, what can I tell you?
The wind blows through your sleep
You dream proverbial dreams

We are now

III

The moon in her first quarter gone and the wind
now overcast

hidden nostrils, sleeping fingers
hair at a toss on half-pillows
                          bedroom smells

the slow death and the slow birth of cells
seepage of time; no wonder dreams

fail us, no
telling the true figures the dead left

IV

I repaired the burnt-out room at last
covered the charred rafters with
asbestos sheet and a gallon of white paint

a bed and a rush mat
two chairs, a desk, a bookcase
keep it simple –

the sun by day, the wind by night
reviving the dead-world. Your long journey through the dark
never ends, clock

no count, silver and black
the great circle wheels through the stars –

our words leave shadows where they fall.

Moby

One day I got up and found my cock was gone. My dream told me nothing. I had been hot, and taken a swim, but there were no sharks, nothing, no crocodiles, nothing, no piranhas. It had not swum off by itself. I checked every hole in the house, rat hole, mouse hole, plug, socket, tap, drain, vent, the cap of my pen, the car exhaust, all the locks. Absent. There was a strange emanation of semen in the room but nothing to account for it. My doctor was on holiday. My wife had no suggestions. There was no wound, no slash, cut or recent scar. All my fingers were fingers, all my toes were toes, the breakfast sausages were all accounted for. There was, in other words, no tranference, no substitution, no masquerade. I thought of the tomb and the three days and wondered if I would see it again, risen, the hole in its side, the stigmata. It had been a perfectly good, functional, working cock, no avatar of anything higher, not at any time I knew it. And what concerned me most was one of my exits had been cut off, removed, though I couldn't even infer that for there was no evidence of any agent, interference, theft. With nothing to go on, complain of, I decided the manly thing to do was to sit back and wait until the thing came back of its own accord. The only point that bothered me was what the thing might be doing off there by itself, without a guiding intelligence. For certain it must be hunting some female, of what species I couldn't, daren't, guess. And what would it bring back? Or what, without my knowledge, would it inseminate and give rise to? What mutant? I was surprised how responsible I felt about this. A man attached to his cock can screw who he likes. But the promiscuity, the impropriety, of what my cock might do by itself *in my name* made me feel faint with responsibility. For a man can care less what he does in his own person: this was a matter of social principle, an outrage, felony. If every man's cock demanded its freedom, equality, parity, took it, where would the race be? We would be a new proletariat, slaving to support our cocks in their search for freedom.

Egg

A white room filled with wind –
this is the Buddha

                    but wind
being movement
defies being named

is not particles of time and matter
it touches: leaf, fur and lake
survive
to go their own ways

colors change

white remains
the moon and stars

a white room with the stillness of
no wind,
            the silence
Pindar feared –

the death of words   by definition

time

Hardware

Out in space, the few
fiery particles of man
circle without water
or in free fall

dream of gravity
unhinged
polished by sunlight
some movement, even the sense of

going somewhere
some notion of height or speed
out of touch
even with the sun

who can't melt them down
or do anything with them
and the moon
whose breast-feeding days are past

forgotten
in the earth-mind
unknown to the other minds
earth cannot know

yet with our fingerprints
and perhaps a ghost of an odor left
of sweat and oil
angelic, if metal were bone

and can some star in space
bless these, which are all we have
that muscled our way out of the slime
into starlight, hoping?

Fa-yung

Were you lonely on the mountain?

Immaterial
the wind
      the stars
the people you have left
the ant cars filing towards their nest

To meditate
the body must leave
                dance, without gravity
yet as if an iron rod
impaled you
      held you
stiff, like a sample butterfly
or a dying convict on a Turkish bridge

No song
to accompany you . . .
just highlands, and further highlands of cloud

and you think you have touched your mind

Look at yourself
with heaven's eye
how small in the scale of creation
                you dwindle
in search of that final cell

the universe.

Dead One

By that time, I just wanted a little peace and quiet. I had my vanities. My wigs. My dresses. My face. Certain opinions people held to be vanities, which were just my uncertainties, really, and a certain brightness of saying them. I had my small passions, netsuke, little ivory walnuts, children, animals, grace in welcoming strangers. If my grand manner was not working so well now, it was because I saw I could not hold onto things. People were my passion and I could not change. It was amazing how suddenly my magic went, after you went, and you went, and no one else came, and when I cried for help the cracked hag voices of former confessors and friends were not on the phone, began to talk about me behind my back and to my face as Anna Karenina or the demon mistress, whoever happened to suit their demonology of the moment and salvage their straight selves all striving to be good people and saints after lives that contradicted that. Take it from me, all women are grasping. Not all bitches by any means, but the worst ones are not and grab the hardest, being good and true to themselves, destroy you by shrinking you down, asking you to answer their fundamental questions when you are already too far gone in the wrong vis a vis them to answer them honestly, for that would not be taken kindly either, and what claim have they to be your conscience? I warned you, go to America, I think you have better sense. Don't get trapped in claims of the absolute, for you are the absolute, as much as any that exist, stop trying to preserve your soul. Be your cold self until someone warms you. I could say this now you were gone. I can say this now I am gone, and have invented this life for you, where you wander without my cunning, with your hard innocence that falsifies things. I died in the hell you warned me about and half created for me, with what fondness, what loathing, what tears. You remember a snowfield at Christmas, a big house full of many languages, where you lifted me up and carried me naked to an open window to look at the moonlight. Still, frozen picture. No energy, no future. I have always been afraid of the snow.

Here I am. Here. A voice talking, out of a snow-drift, maimed beyond any further fear. By that time, I just wanted a little peace and quiet. And they talked of their sickness, and how they could not help me, not just now, but wait a little, not now. And you were the worst because you never came, you never forgave, your inert self in deadlock with the world, my mourning dove, in deadlock with the world. And all the time we knew each other best and could not say anything. But how free we were to say everything! if you had cared. The slow clock crawls backwards to a jangling morning alarm. I see you walking east over a snowfield, towards a spirit you will never understand, not in the day or in the night, but in a mid-world of cold, that day of the northern year when the sun never comes. You are still looking for what we could not find, and I have had to find alone. Is this what you wanted? Was that it? But you have (rumor reaches through the roots) found something else, something quite different. I'm so restless, so cold. I must see. Please give me eyes. Give me back my eyes. A woman can't live alone. She is only half herself, by herself. My restless half wanders like Cain over the earth through chinatown the mountains the harbour, through vague religions, round and round, like a frog with a crushed leg, wherever you are, morning sickness, wherever you are, terrified of your own words, your cold self, wandering. I will reach you at night when you are still. They said, be patient, it is we who are sick, not you. Give us a little time to compose our minds and we will help you. Backing away, backing through the eyes, away. For the trail of sickness lies not through the sick but through the strong, they did not want me. They wanted their mothers, fathers, sisters, brothers, friends, but not me. You see, it is not only you I must talk to. And the clutter and mess and rubbish I left is all the self they left me . . . impermanent, as Nagasena said, part of the flux. How easily the self slips away when approached, pinned, with the final question. This is me speaking, Me. The name I was given, the name you took away. I came, wanting to talk to you. You were very polite. You had no place for me to stay. You took me to a room they had

57

prepared for me. It was underground, and the walls were made of iron, the door locked on the outside. We both knew what the room was; but I only smiled, and you said I have to go now, and left me there with that fake blessing of your raised hand, walked out into life without turning back to look while I started to arrange the bed and said goodnight to myself, a prayer that I would see daylight again though I knew that was not likely, as Nagasena said, perhaps we care too much for such things. You turned away from my death as you have from everything else, with what pain I do not know, with what indifference. A season has gone by since I last talked to you. Wind stirs the tree whose root nudges my left side. You do not come.

Lament

> She chose
> the sun for myth
> in a land where snowdrops thrive
> on cold and water,
>
> fine bones
> showing the skull,
> leaf-skeleton
> longer than any summer:
>
> one would not know
> how fine her waiting, her
> sorrow, the gestures of life
> kept to the end

October

You dream about circuses, the clown, the tightrope walker,
heights, and falls, drums and horns,
sequined bareback riders,
ringmasters with whips
                        the smoky tent
of autumn, nights
of dim lamps and sawdust, tumblers and acrobats
circling you, through fiery hoops
                        putting you through your paces,
glare-red eyes
at whip-touch,
                and the dead faces
                        under the great cone of smoke
applaud you
or jeer you —
you are one unlisted, your act begins in silence
you wait for the end of night, biding your time
                                their attention
desperately, yours,
                for the sun to rise,
sorcery of the will, for the sun to rise
burning out the canvas sky, cone
                        of smoke, dim light —
for theirs is another age
a time before sunrise
and you must see them die in the great fire of your will
                                under the hooves
of the scared beasts
you have started —

to begin at sunrise imitating the birds
to lie under the leaves that hide the stars

Sickness

You turn
in the green circle of fever
at grass
        above your grave
beneath the sun

between
ice-age and tropic
talking new life into the earth
              burn and cool

dancing in the moon
the hot evening star
        and the cooler star of morning
murmurs

of cold sea
the sweat-bed ocean sand
where the drowned airman lay wrapped
                 in his parachute
eyes on the hidden stars

two hundred feet of darkness

there, for a time
mollusc
to your revival and play in the dry
             winds of Wyoming
shell-beds, hills

I wait for your journey to end
for the sun to draw your poisons

we who have no gods but keep returning.

Creek

Rivers asleep in the rock
broken eyes
now they are awakening
colors
salmon and leaf
threading
the sky: illusion above where
no light can reach
salmon, leaf
wonder of spines
that bend like water
slipping through life as water
now
they are awakening, tongues
the old ferns
hazel, buckeye, alders, rainbells
trilliums, catkins, polypores
ferns with licorice roots
adder's tongue, burl
in the rain bracken
smells
redds in the gravel sleek
strong spines bending as water
heal this hurt spine
heal
this winnowing of children
make new lives
from the snowtops to the sea
asleep in rock
awakening eyes
colors
the light can reach

From a Yoruba Poem

The light-beast rose early
stepped, like the duyker
'Shaking the grass like bells'

in the garden, by the water pail
where the coral snake lived
under stones soaked
by the dripping tap

euh! euh! the deaf-mute
deer-sound, so like a young goat
born in a dry-season ditch

I wish I could talk like that

spare word that needs no mirror
that does not dance for itself
but steps
'shaking the grass like bells'

in the heart of the hunter
who knows
what it is he must kill, preserve

of life
for life to return, rising early
to catch the light-beast in the grass
before his shadow crosses it

Live One

I was waiting for my self to return and tell me what I desired.
I was not afraid of the unknown, but was haunted by the known.
I could not relate my parts together, I could not balance the
needle of self between the extremes of my inconsistencies. I was
like a collection of little, insignificant things found in the pockets
of a dead man: a watch, a pencil stub, coins, phone numbers, a
half-smoked cigarette, an empty wallet, photographs, dust. I
lacked the thread to tie these things together and identify myself.
The deep river had washed over me, I was bloated and without
feelings. I could not tell anyone anything about myself, and was
waiting for future events to define me. I knew I was afraid of
the people I had known, more than anything, that they had some
thread of me I did not have, and that that thread was not the
true one, because as they pulled on it I felt my self unravel,
whereas the thread I had to find would tie me together, restore
my pattern. People looked at me with knowing looks. You are
sick, put your self in our hands, and we will heal you. And they
did not know how much I feared their looks, their hands, their
voices. They did not know how far back I had to go, so far
beyond them, how far forward I had to reach, where they did
not even exist, and how light I had to travel, through light,
through utter blankness where there was no shadow but mine.
To get there I had to snap their sticky webs clinging to me, and
they cried in pain, faint cries of the betrayed spider as my wings
they did not believe I could use beat me free. And free was no-
where. Free was the possibility of everywhere. I was rebuked
by what I had touched, like a whale scarred by the disks of a
giant squid. I was scarred with the signs of my struggle and
capture, an imperfect, flawed creature swimming through light
in search of its lost parts. Then I found you

And you were you.

You were what I wanted. You loved me, lying inside me that
first time that sunlit evening in January, lit by the westward
light, your scars melting, you looked at me and said

I was waiting for my self to return and tell me what I desired. I was not afraid of the unknown, but was haunted by the known. I could not relate my parts together, I could not balance the needle of self between the extremes of my inconsistencies. I was like a collection of little, insignificant things found in the pockets of a dead man: a watch, a pencil stub, coins, phone numbers, a half-smoked cigarette, an empty wallet, photographs, dust. I lacked the thread to tie these things together and identify myself. The deep river had washed over me, I was bloated and without feelings. I could not tell anyone anything about myself, and was waiting for future events to define me. I knew I was afraid of the people I had known, more than anything, that they had some thread of me I did not have, and that that thread was not the true one, because as they pulled on it I felt my self unravel, whereas the thread I had to find would tie me together, restore my pattern. People looked at me with knowing looks. You are sick, put yourself in our hands, and we will heal you. And they did not know how much I feared their looks, their hands, their voices. They did not know how far back I had to go, so far beyond them, how far forward I had to reach, where they did not even exist, and how light I had to travel, through light, through utter blankness where there was no shadow but mine. To get there I had to snap their sticky webs clinging to me, and they cried in pain, faint cries of the betrayed spider as my wings they did not believe I could use beat me free. And free was no-where. Free was the possibility of everywhere. I was rebuked by what I had touched, like a whale scarred by the disks of a giant squid. I was scarred with the signs of my struggle and capture, an imperfect, flawed creature swimming through light in search of its lost parts.

Then I found you

The Geometry of the Blind

And he said –
truth's no crucible
          precipitate
boiled
from the blood

        wind is a fact
heat
we have eyes everywhere
but from zero to one
know
ignorance

  II
The journey through the day
and the journey through night

a man in two minds
        with one eye –
and the adversary
is dark or bright

is neither you

  III
My legs have been my eyes
My fingertips have been my brain

Here comes God
        on his tricycle

with a message

from mother

IV

The opposite of now
is now
      not when

pain is burning
joy is burning

learn, love

you are wiser than I am

ten years between us
taught me how to lie

V

And if I talk about the dead as
failed selves
        that is because
I possess them now, they
wake into my life –
          and I turn
to the strong sun
    asking what they were

that they should be

VI

Bird in space
   the sculptor's blade
is metal
the edge of fire

                    sight

        always beyond the visible

        blind child,
        before nearing us

        let love be in us

        shape your creator's hand

For Sharon

            Now they begin to stare
            through your clothes
            at the skin's
            underthings, your rounding belly

            a long waiting
            until the form beside you becomes
            another
                    to smell the wind, learn
            the stillness in things then
            how they are put together

            how the parts move

            and mornings are
            a year
                    how all things move, leaf
            a fallen angel, turds
            the self's homage to earth

before other signs

How I make myself
still

eyes
preparing an image
to greet what comes with one more whole
                              than itself
a man
and father